T0276585

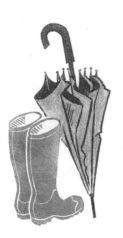

"A change in the weather is sufficient to recreate the world and ourselves."

Marcel Proust

WILD
WEATHER

The Myths, Science and
Wonder of Weather

Alison Davies

Illustrated by Clare Melinksy

Hardie Grant

QUADRILLE

Contents

Introduction

We are shaped by the weather. From the first
tentative rays of sunshine that herald a new day,
to the bracing winds that propel us forwards.
The rain wraps soggy fingers around our
shoulders in a cleansing embrace, and sometimes
shocks us with its urgency, while thunder whips
at our heels and lightning takes our breath away.
Snow falls, bringing with it a blanket of calm,
and we are enchanted by each pretty flake – but
should the snow increase its fervour, then we are
struck dumb. Our awe quickly turns to ice, and
we are chilled to the bone.

Sometimes the heavens greet us with a gift
– a colourful rainbow that sets hearts alight with
hope. Sometimes they challenge us with events
beyond our control: tumbling tornadoes that
tear through the landscape; savage snowdrifts;
never-ending floods; droughts that bleed the
earth to a husk. The elements craft our fate and
we stand helpless, at the mercy of the weather's
demeanour, hoping for the best, preparing for
the worst.

*"Climate is what we expect,
weather is what we get."*

Mark Twain

Each meteorological marvel has its place and brings blessings that we can enjoy and work with. Like the entities and beings that control the elements in folk tales and mythology, each weather condition has a magic, which is unlocked in the pages of this book. Travel through the ages and discover what the Ancients saw and how they interpreted the winds and the rain, the glorious light of the sun and the unforgiving chill of winter. Learn too, how such phenomenons exist, what wonders lie behind the making of these things and read about real-life wild weather events that have changed the world. As you unravel the secrets of the skies you will see that we are all connected through the power of Mother Nature, and you will recognize the role she plays in sculpting life today. More importantly, you will understand how the intricate dance of the climate moulds the future of our planet.

Take a journey through the pages of this book and you will learn the secrets of the weather, why we need each meteorological front and how it helps us as a planet. You'll discover the myths and legends, and the science behind it all. More importantly, you'll see the interaction between human and nature, and how you can embrace the elemental changes and connect with their power. Each season has something to celebrate, a gift that can enhance your life. The more you understand the weather and how it works, the more you can harness its individual energy. Take a peek outside your window, dress accordingly and get up close and personal with *Wild Weather*.

SUNSHINE
AND RAINBOWS

Sunshine and rainbows

When the sun shines, the heavens smile. The sky, framed in light, becomes a glorious streak of endless blue, and the earth lets out a breath. The bounty of the burning orb is never-ending. It sustains and nurtures, warms and thrills. The sweetest kiss of sunshine is enough to melt the hardest heart, lifting spirits and layers as it turns up the heat. It doesn't matter who or where you are, there's no escape from the sun's charms, for its rays reach out to enfold even the smallest and most invisible micro-organism.

Yes, the sun is all consuming, but it is also fiery – let us not forget its true nature or the extreme lengths of its power. If the sun has you in its sights, then there is no escape. The land will dry and crack, its brittle surface splintered and gaping, waiting for rain to quench the thirst. The trees and plants will wither and die, and all life will crumble; such is the searing might of this glowing ball.

Lucky, then, that the sun is a generous leader, a father and a deity, a prize to be claimed and carried as precious cargo through the sky in mythologies around the world.

Escorted by gods and angels, chased by demons and mythical creatures, it is a magical force from which the Ancients of this world drew their power and strength. Universally worshipped and admired, and set high in the sky to command our attention, the sun is an integral part of who we are and our survival.

Even without its life-giving power, we can embrace its energy. On those days when life is tough and our hearts are heavy, a glimpse of sunshine can make all the difference. The reassuring sight of this circle of light above our heads, is enough to raise a smile, to lift the spirits and make you feel lucky to be alive. Long may it shine!

*"The sun does not shine
for a few trees
and flowers, but the
wide world's joy."*

Henry Ward Beecher

Sunshine explained

The sun and the seasons

With a magnetic field that extends to the very edges of the solar system, the sun is more than just a fiery ball. Its impact upon the earth is colossal, affecting the tides and warming the seas, triggering the shift in seasons and weather patterns and assisting in the growth of vegetation. It is at the centre of each season, for as the earth moves it spins upon its axis and different parts of the globe are exposed to the light, giving rise to spring, summer, autumn and winter. When the sun's path in the sky is at its furthest north or furthest south, we experience the shortest day of the year, known as the winter solstice, and the longest, known as the summer solstice.

Equinoxes

Twice a year, during the spring and autumn, an equinox occurs, and the earth is split in two, with equal amounts of day and night. The planet, which usually orbits the sun on an axis of 23.5 degrees, shifts so that the sun sits neatly above the equator, providing almost perfect balance. This casts a dividing line between light and dark and indicates the shift as we move from one season to another.

Solar cycles

The sun, being a hot ball of charged gas, moves through a cycle, just as the seasons roll on. Every 11 years, the magnetic field of this blazing orb switches things up, so that north becomes south and vice versa. It then takes another 11 years to change back. The surface of the sun reflects these changes, with the appearance of sunspots, which increase throughout the cycle. At the beginning there are very few, by the middle the surface could be littered, and they gradually fade out towards the end.

Ancient Chinese astrologers were the first to record sunspots, during the Shang dynasty, and it was soon recognized that the more prolific they were, the more solar power would hit the earth's atmosphere. Essential and all consuming, the sun was a beacon for those early people. A central point of worship. A power that could not be controlled, only monitored and followed.

Solar eclipse

A solar eclipse occurs when the moon lines up with the earth and sun during its monthly orbit and casts shadows on the earth's surface. The sun's diameter is roughly 400 times bigger than the moon, and the sun is around 400 times further away, which is why they appear almost the same size in the sky. An eclipse can only happen during a new moon phase, as this is the time the moon passes in between the earth and the sun. The position of the moon must be exact and in perfect alignment to create this phenomenon. There are at least two solar eclipses every year, although they may be partial – a total eclipse is a much rarer event.

Droughts

Considered one of the worse natural disasters of the world, a drought is defined as a period of time – which could be a season, a year, or several years – of extremely dry weather and low precipitation. This results in a severe water shortage, which in turn causes crops to fail, livestock to die, and widespread famine. Fluctuating weather patterns are to blame, although there is evidence that climate change plays a significant role in these catastrophes.

Rainbows explained

Optical illusion

They look like pure magic, but rainbows are an optical illusion caused when light passes through water droplets hanging in the air. The waves of white light are refracted (change direction) as they pass through the water, are then reflected off the back of the droplet and refracted again as they exit. This causes the light to bounce off in different directions that appear as several different colours to the human eye – the individual waves of colour vary in wavelength and this is what produces the differing hues. Red has the longest wavelength, bending at a 42-degree angle, and because of this, red commonly appears on the outer edge of the rainbow. Violet light has the shortest wavelength, bending at around 40 degrees, so it usually appears on the inner edge of the rainbow. A double rainbow is when a lighter rainbow appears above the first rainbow, caused by a double reflection of light – which also explains why the colour order is reversed. While rainbows can appear close or far away, they are not tied to a particular location. The position of the observer in relation to the direction of light determines the appearance of the location.

Folklore and superstition

Sunshine

Solar eclipse

The disappearance of the sun from the sky caused the Ancients to come up with a number of creative theories to explain what was happening. To them it appeared that the sun had either been swallowed by some otherworldly beast or stolen by magical trickery. In some mythologies they did their best to chase away the ghastly beings that would steal their light, by banging drums and making as much noise as possible to scare them.

In Vietnam a giant celestial frog or toad was accused of swallowing the sun whole, while the Kwakiutl tribe of western Canada attributed the blame to the mouth of heaven, which hungrily swallows the sun or moon during an eclipse. In Hindu mythology the greedy demon Rahu disguises himself as a god, so that he can drink the elixir of immortality. Unfortunately, his plan is scuppered by the sun and moon, who tell the great god Vishnu. Rahu manages only the briefest sip of the elixir before Vishnu chops off his head. As the magical liquid doesn't have time to reach his body it dies, but his head remains alive and travels through the sky, chasing the sun and moon as revenge. Sometimes the demon gets so close that he manages to swallow the sun, causing an eclipse, but having no throat the sun drops easily from his grasp and back to its seat in the sky. The Navajo regard an eclipse as a sacred time, when balance is restored to the earth. They mark this event by singing songs and telling stories in their family groups.

Red sky at night

While the phrase 'Red sky at night, shepherd's delight. Red sky in the morning, shepherd's warning' is a quirky, and popular superstition, there is truth to the folklore. The rosy evening glow is created when dust particles are trapped in the atmosphere by a wave of high pressure, meaning fair weather is moving in the next day. When this red sky appears in the morning, the high pressure has slipped away.

Myths and magic

Rainbows

One of life's true joys, the rainbow arcs in the sky for all to see – a symbol of light after darkness, of hope after the floods, with a long history throughout humanity. According to the Bible, the rainbow was a sign from God that he would never flood the earth again.

Today, the sight of a rainbow can stop us in our tracks. It's a feel-good moment, a gift from Mother Nature and enough to turn any frown upside down. While it might not be key to existence, it reminds us to look up, to appreciate the

wonder in the world, and that is sometimes all we need to make a difference. The word itself comes from the Latin *arcus pluvius*, which means 'rainy arch', and although a prominent symbol in myths and religions for thousands of years, nobody really understood what it was, until the 17th century.

In folklore, it's referred to as the rainbow bridge, a potent symbol associated with good fortune. With a pretty blend of colours splashed across the sky, it lifts the spirits and offers the promise of something magical that can only be found at its end. While it might be impossible to arrive at this destination, Ancients from around the world have tried, building tales and myths to help explain the mystery of this phenomenon.

In Norse mythology a rainbow bridge, by the name of Bifrost, provides passage from earth to Asgard, the realm of the gods. It is the only way to reach this hallowed place and can be accessed by gods and the souls of brave warriors. To the Irish the rainbow is a lucky omen, for there is a pot brimming with gold at the end – along with a leprechaun guard. The Hindu god Indra wields a heavenly rainbow to fire arrows of lightning at the demon serpent Asura Vritra. In Armenian mythology, the rainbow is the belt of the sun god Tir, while Bulgarian legend suggests that a rainbow has the power to transform mankind by changing the sex of the person who walks beneath it: the belief is that a man who walks beneath the light of a rainbow will think and act like a woman, and a woman who does the same will become more manly!

While most rainbow folklore is positive, some mythologies take a dim view of this vibrant spectacle. The Amazonians believed that rainbows were evil spirits sent to torment them. These harmful entities caused miscarriages and sickness, and to avoid ill fortune it was common practice to shut your mouth at the sight of a rainbow to prevent infection. In ancient Japan, the rainbow was thought to represent a giant snake, while the ancient Slavs believed that if you were touched by a rainbow you would turn into a half demon, known as a Planetnik.

Deities

Sunshine

Without the sun there would be no life on earth. This ball of fire that sits in the sky is our salvation. It provides much needed light and energy for the plants which in turn sustain us, and every creature upon the planet. It generates weather patterns, affects the tides, and its shifting position and temperature aids migration. The sun is at the heart of who we are, and this is why ancient peoples from around the world revered it. They understood its power and gave it magical significance, believing it to have 'god-like' status.

Radiant and all-powerful, sun deities were worshipped for their warmth and energy. Unlike other gods and goddesses they consistently rewarded their people with light, warmth and an abundance of healthy crops. The common thread from around the world is the sun's daily journey through the sky, and each mythology has a way of explaining this – along with other phenomena like an eclipse or the seasonal shift between summer and winter.

The sun, like the earth, is ever changing. Ancient scholars would have observed these astronomical mood swings and the effects they had upon the landscape, from the dramatic shifts in temperature to lights in the sky. Everything was noted, read and seen as an omen from the Gods.

Apollo

With film star good looks and an athletic build, Apollo is one of the most popular Greek gods. A sun deity first and foremost, he is also associated with light, healing, prophecy, music and poetry. Being a son of Zeus, he is right up there with the elite of his kind. As patron of music and poetry, he is also the leader of the muses. While he has many healing gifts, he can also bring illness and plague, depending on his mood.

Ra

The Egyptian sun god Ra is thought to be the creator of earth and all life, making him of supreme importance to his people – many solar temples were built in his honour and the rays of the sun throughout the day were believed to be a manifestation of his power. Travelling through the sky with the demon serpent Apep in hot pursuit, Ra is swallowed each night by the sky goddess Nut and taken to the Underworld, then reborn again each dawn to fight another day. His symbol is a giant sun dial that he wears as part of his headdress. In artwork he is often depicted with the head of a falcon.

Amaterasu

This gorgeous Japanese sun goddess has a heart of gold and cares deeply for her people. When her selfish brother Susanoo, the storm god, went on a destructive rampage throughout the land, Amaterasu was devastated and hid away in a cave. Broken-hearted, she refused to come out, and the land was plunged into darkness. Crops failed and the world became a cold and shadowy place. Luckily, after petitions by the other gods, Amaterasu was lured from hiding by the goddess Amenouzume, who performed an outrageous dance outside the cave. She made such a noise that it piqued Amaterasu's curiosity and she emerged into the outside world, bringing the sunlight with her. This was the start of brighter summer days after a long harsh winter.

Belenus

A powerful Celtic sun god worshipped throughout Europe, the name Belenus means 'the shining god'. According to legend, he rides through the sky on his chariot, with the sun in tow. Sometimes he is pictured throwing lightning bolts and using a giant wheel as a shield. He is associated with the Celtic festival Beltane, held on the first day of May – the 'fires of bel' were lit during this celebration as a way of marking the sun's return to the sky.

Sunna

Sunna, also known as Sol, is the Norse goddess of the sun. Each morning she begins her journey across the sky in a chariot pulled by the horses Alsvin, meaning 'very fast', and Arvakr, which means 'early rising'. These powerful beasts gallop at lightning speed, which is just as well because they are being chased by the hungry wolf Skoll. When he gets too close he nips at the sun, taking a small bite and causing an eclipse.

Rainbows

Australian Rainbow Serpent

Known as Ngalyod in the Kuninjku language of Arnhem Land, the Rainbow Serpent is associated with all forms of water, from creeks and lakes to water holes, and also water plants like lilies, vines and palms. Recognized by the Aborigines as the great giver of life and linked to renewal, the Rainbow Serpent sheds its skin to be reborn again. With the ability to whip up a storm and control rainfall, this powerful creature is revered and honoured. Those who wish to speak to it, and elicit favour, will sit and sing by a water hole in the hope that it hears their message. While it brings many blessings to the world, it can also cause droughts if offended by humankind. Living beneath the earth, the Rainbow Serpent travels between water holes and also in storm clouds.

Iris

The glorious Greek goddess Iris gained her name from the Greek word for 'rainbow'. Daughter of the Titan god Thaumas and his oceanic cloud nymph wife Elektra, Iris is often seen clasping a pitcher of water, which she carries to the heavens. The ancient Greeks considered her a messenger between gods and mortals, simply because of the way a rainbow connects heaven and earth. Like her male counterpart Hermes, Iris has wings and carries a staff. Described as 'swift footed', Iris is the deity of choice when it comes to delivering and transcribing messages from the gods. Like the beautiful rainbows that follow in her wake, she is considered one of the prettiest deities of the time.

Did you know?

Longest lasting rainbow
The world's longest lasting rainbow to date
occurred on Thursday November 30, 2017, over
northern Taiwan. The rainbow, which first appeared
at 6.57am and lasted till 3.55pm the same day,
stretched ribbons of colour across the sky for almost
nine hours, delighting those who managed to take a
snap of the phenomenon. Experts believe a seasonal
monsoon trapped moisture in the air, forming clouds
and sunshine, while a slow and steady wind speed
contributed to the spectacle. Rainbows typically last
just under an hour.

RE-WILD:

Make your own sun dial

Tell the time of day by using the position of the sun in the sky. As the sun shines throughout the day, a shadow is cast in different places on your sun dial, and you can read this to tell the time like the early civilizations would have done.

You'll need a stick around 60cm (23in) in length and a handful of stones or crystals to mark each hour of the dial.

1. Find a patch of grass that is exposed to the sun for most of the day and position your stick in the earth. If you live in the northern hemisphere, tilt it to the north, and if you live in the southern hemisphere, tilt towards the south.

2. Start early in the morning when the sun has just risen. Look at your clock when it is 7am and see where the stick casts a shadow, then mark this spot with a stone.

3. Every hour, on the hour, check where the shadow is pointing and leave a stone to mark the spot.

4. Continue until the sun sets, and you'll be left with the perfect sun dial.

RE-WILD:

Connect with the life-giving
energy of the sun

The sun is the key to everything. Every culture
and tribe, every seed, sapling and shrub. Every
creature that walks the earth feels its benevolent
heat and benefits from the warmth that it brings.
It dictates the change in seasons, the length of
days and the way we feel. Our spirits are lifted
when we see it shining brightly and the briefest
kiss of sunlight can turn a frown upside down;
no wonder, then, that it's associated with the
essence of joy. As humans we spend much of
our time in search of blissful serenity when
the answer is staring down at us from the sky.
All you have to do is harness the sun's radiant
energy, to release your inner happiness.

1. Find a comfortable spot outside where you
   can watch the sunrise.

2. Have a few moments of quiet contemplation
   and consider all the things in your life that
   bring you happiness, and all the blessings
   you are thankful for.

3. Relax and watch as the sun begins to transform the sky.

4. Feel each colour as it emerges, and blends into the view.

5. Take your time and breathe it in.

6. Notice how the light and heat transform the earth, changing the way it looks and feels.

7. Imagine the sun slowly rising within your chest. Each time you inhale, it gets bigger and brighter, until it floods your entire body with warmth.

8. Let those feelings of joy permeate every part of you, and as you exhale, release the light through each pore.

WIND

Wind

On a hot summer's day there is nothing more welcoming than the wind's soft embrace.
A conduit to melody, it entertains us by bringing bird song and far away laughter, the peaceful rustle of the swaying trees and the scent of roses in full bloom. The gentle kiss of a summer's breeze is the kindest gift. Like a lover's tender touch, it elevates the spirits and whispers sweet nothings as it curls around the ear.

During those fresh autumnal months it whips the leaves into a frenzy, and we marvel as they dance before our eyes. The trees, now much starker than before, act as buffers as it fires hearty gusts in their direction. We, too, feel the power building, the force that blows through our hair and wraps us in a nippy cloak of air. For when the wind blusters there is nowhere to hide.
At the full height of its power we are defenceless. It tears through the landscape, clawing with unseen hands at anything left exposed. It rips and destroys, batters and breaks, like an invisible giant bent on destruction. The tirade cannot be calmed, until the giant has his fill.

The Ancients were in awe of the cleansing might of the wind, believing that the gods were responsible and imbuing this force of nature with

supernatural gifts. They attempted to appease the beast with rituals and spells, and sometimes sought its aid when navigating the high seas. The wind, like any form of weather, has highs and lows; it is a tempestuous entity that cannot be tamed, and yet, as humans, we still try to harness its power.

Messenger gods of old were often associated with the wind's power. After all, this mighty force plays an important role in spreading the life-giving heat of the sun throughout the earth. It also spirits away pollution, helping to cleanse the atmosphere. Like any swift messenger, it's always on hand to deliver what we need, to aid our survival – even more so today, as we work with wind power in a bid to combat climate change. The wind is a trusty weather warrior, always present and ready to propel us forwards.

"At the heart of the cyclone tearing the sky is a place of central calm."

Edwin Markham

The wind explained

Whirlwinds

Whirlwinds, which include tornadoes and waterspouts, are caused by changes in atmospheric pressure that whip up into a vortex of wind. Varying in size, whirlwinds can be anything from small dust devils to destructive tornadoes that spread for several miles. Depending on its size, the vertical column of frenzied air often picks up debris as it swirls its way across the land – anything from dust, leaves, and even fish have been claimed by the powerful gusts. Flames, too, can be whipped up if the whirlwind is close to a wildfire; this results in fire whirls.

There are two categories of whirlwind, major and minor, depending on the intensity and speed of the wind. Minor whirlwinds are made up of spiralling local winds that create a funnel, while major whirlwinds are created when a condensation funnel forms beneath cumuliform clouds; this happens during supercell thunderstorms. The funnel contains winds that can travel up to 110 miles (177 kilometres) per hour, and some of the worst become thrashing tornadoes with wind speeds that exceed 200 miles (322 kilometres) per hour. Waterspouts also fall into this category; these marine-based whirlwinds are responsible for the phenomenon of 'raining fish'. The powerful vortex sucks the fish up into the air, and then carries them closer to the shore, before releasing them in a flurry from the heavens. While not as destructive as tornadoes, waterspouts can still be devastating. Hundreds of deaths were caused when one exceptional waterspout struck the Grand Harbour in Valletta, Malta in 1555.

How wind is made

Wind is created when the sun heats one part of the atmosphere differently from another. This causes expansion of the warmer air, creating less pressure where it is warm

than where it is cold. Air moves from high pressure to low pressure, and this movement of air is wind.

A strong sea breeze is present because the sun heats the air above land quicker than the air above water. The warm air then expands and rises, and the cooler air from the ocean pushes towards the land to take the place of the rising air.

Hurricanes

Originating in the Atlantic Basin, which includes the Atlantic Ocean, Caribbean Sea, Gulf of Mexico, and the eastern and central North Pacific Ocean, hurricanes are tropical cyclones that occur over tropical and sub-tropical waters. When a storm's maximum sustained winds reach 74 miles (119 kilometres) per hour, it is categorized as a hurricane – anything less than this is a tropical storm.

Myths and magic

On a windy day, there's nothing more refreshing than standing in the flow of a gust, and letting it blow away the cobwebs, but the cleansing energy of the wind has as much to do with the warmth of the sun as it does the cold air. These two dance partners cavort together in the sky, to create this phenomenon. It may have looked like magic to our ancestors, but to us it's the perfect partnership and a key element of the weather cycle.

Ancient mystics noted not only the direction of the wind, but also its strength, attributing these traits once more to the Gods. A fast and furious force, that would appear to come from nowhere, it's no wonder the wind was associated with messenger deities. The velocity and direction of each gust contributed to its character, and so specific winds had different names.

In Greek mythology the four winds, one for each cardinal direction, are collectively called the Anemoi. They are the sons of Eos, the goddess of the dawn, and Astraeus the god of the dusk. Boreas is the north wind, Zephyros the west, Notos the south and Euros the east. Each is associated with a season: Boreas, the most notable and powerful, being winter; Zephyros is the gentle god of spring breezes; Notos is responsible for summer storms; Euros is associated with autumn. Descriptions of the winds vary – some say they are man-shaped beings with wings who live on Mount Haimos;

others refer to them as muscular stallions with flowing manes that are stabled on the island of Aiolos and are put out to graze along the earth's shore. The Aellai Harpyiai, otherwise known as the Harpies, are the female equivalent of the four winds, and their consorts, while the Venti are their Roman counterparts.

Deities

Like the gales they wield with spectral fingers, gods of the wind are passionate by nature, quick to anger, but just as fast to calm. They twist the air to suit their needs and moods. Ever present like the air we breathe, they watch over us, providing protection when it's needed but also chastising. Wind deities were always a favourite of storytellers, who worked with the changing nature of the elements to spin epic tales of war and peace.

Amun

One of the earliest Egyptian gods, Amun is one of the deities responsible for the creation of the world. His name, which can be spelled many ways, translates to 'Hidden One', which refers to his power over the wind and air. He is usually depicted as a bearded man sitting upon a throne and holding an ankh in one hand and a sceptre in the other. He can also appear as a goose – in this form he is known as 'the Great Cackler' – or in the shape of a man with the head of a frog or snake.

Stribog

This supreme god of the ancient Slavs is a powerful wind deity. Able to inhabit any space, from the tiniest hole to the tallest mountain, he was born from the sparks of the heavenly smith's hammer as it hit the Alatir stone. Usually appearing as an old man with a long white beard and a

bow in his hands, he also carries a golden horn that he uses to summon the winds. Depending on his mood, which is usually miserable, he can conjure anything from a pleasant breeze to a powerful storm.

Feng Popo

This Chinese wind goddess, also known as 'Madame Wind', is wizened and crone-like in appearance. She may be old, but her years give her much wisdom and with this she is able to balance the elements and assist humankind. However, like many wind deities, she is temperamental and likes to unleash her wrath upon the earth from time to time in the form of violent storms. She rides through the sky on the back of a giant tiger, tightly gripping a sack full of wind.

Early civilizations recognized the power of the wind and harnessed this energy to help them work the land. As early as 200BC, wind was used to grind grain and pump water. Windmills were a common sight across Europe, over 200 years ago. Originally developed in Persia, the trusty windmill was a powerhouse of energy and an essential farming tool. While the wind's energy was a blessing to most, like all nature there is always a flip side, which when unleashed creates mayhem.

Njord

Norse god of the wind, sea and seafarers, Njord is also the leader of the Vanir – a second race of gods who went to war against the Aesir. Although he was taken hostage in Asgard, Njord soon became a trusted member of the elite gods and a favourite of the great god Odin. With the power to control the winds he is able to calm the seas and quell fires, or bring down the wrath of the heavens upon earth. Associated with abundance and wealth, he is often petitioned for riches. Njord was married to the giantess and goddess of ice and snow, Skadi, but unfortunately the union didn't work out, as neither could decide on where they wanted to live; Skadi loved the snow-capped mountains and Njord preferred the sea. In the end they parted ways.

Oya

Known as 'Lady of the storms', Oya is a Yoruban warrior goddess and the orisha (spirit) of winds and tempests. She governs the realms between life and death and commands the elements; she has the power to conjure the winds, and tornadoes swirl in her wake. The sister-wife of the god of storms, Shango, she walks at his side during thunderstorms. Despite her destructive power she is considered a protective force and is often called upon to settle disputes.

Cyclone Person

According to the Shawnee and Lenape tribes of North America, Cyclone Person is a storm spirit that roams the land. He or she, depending on which tribe you believe, has long whirling tresses that form the tendrils of the tornado.

Despite being the cause of mass destruction, Cyclone Person is a friendly being and is considered a positive omen. The Shawnee note that although tornadoes follow in the wake of this entity, tribal homes and families remain unscathed. They believe this is because Cyclone Person is a kindred spirit.

Whirlwind Woman

To the Native American tribes of the northern plains, Whirlwind Woman is a powerful spirit and a force of nature. A visit from her may bring destruction and chaos, but she is also a gracious being and a giver of visions. Some traditions say she was originally a human girl, whisked from her home by a whirlwind. Other stories describe her as the spirit that lives at the heart of the tornado.

Hecatoncheires

In Greek mythology hurricanes are caused by the Hecatoncheires, three monstrous brothers known as Briareus, Cottus and Gyges. They are the offspring of the sky god Uranus and Gaia the earth goddess. Each hideous brother has fifty heads and a hundred hands, which they used to cause destruction to the world. Uranus, being so appalled by his repugnant offspring, cast them into Tartarus, a grim underworld where chaos reigned. They were eventually rescued by Zeus, who used them in his battle against the Titans. The brothers put their many hands to work, pelting the Titans with rocks until they crumbled. As a reward for their help Zeus gave each a palace under the sea, where they live and punish humankind at the command of the gods.

Did you know?

Fastest wind speed ever recorded
In 2016 scientists discovered wind speeds of up
to 124 million miles (200 million kilometres) per
hour in space. These ultraviolet winds are the
fastest ever recorded in the universe, travelling at
20% of the speed of light around a supermassive
black hole. Space winds are different from the
winds on earth, being made up of jets of plasma
that come from stars like the sun. Quasar winds
are also space winds; these are formed from one
of the four expansive discs of hot air that swirl
around supermassive black holes.

RE-WILD:

Make your own wind chime

Switch off your headphones and instead enjoy the sounds of the wind, by creating a personalized wind chime.

You'll need some strong transparent cord or thread, a small but strong branch and a selection of things to hang from it, like shells, beads, bottle tops, etc.

If you're using shells or bottle tops, you'll need to drill a small hole in them first so that you can hang them.

1. Take several lengths of thread, the same length, and begin threading the shells, beads and bottle tops onto each one. It doesn't matter if they don't match; you can be as creative as you like with the patterns.

2. Secure at one end with a knot or bead, then tie along the length of the branch.

3. Suspend the branch using rope, and let the chimes catch the breeze.

RE-WILD:

Connect with the wind
and release your fear

When the wind whips at your heels, there is
no escape. It's a harsh reminder that you are
exposed to the elements, that no matter where
you are upon the earth, or in your life, you are
vulnerable. Every moment brings change, and
there's nothing like the bristling jolt of a gust
of wind to remind you of this. Just as the wind
berates, it also cajoles you into action, pushing
you onwards through dark clouds and stormy
days. Whether light and breezy, or wild and
wanton, going with the flow of this element
will help you bend and shift with the changes
in your life.

1. On a windy day, find a spot where you can feel the breeze coming at you from all directions. This could be in the middle of a field or park, or high on the peak of a hill.

2. Lift your chin so that your face is turned upwards. Close your eyes and open your arms wide, as if they are two giant wings, and spin around.

3. Feel the wind stroke your cheeks, feel it graze your face, and ruffle your hair. Notice how it curls around your body, nudging you forwards. How does this make you feel? Exhilarated? Excited? Energized?

4. Let your body relax so that it bends and flows in the path of the wind. If time and space allow, you could even open your eyes and run. Let the gusts push and buffet you, in any direction.

5. Imagine you're a leaf being carried through the air and enjoy this feeling of freedom.

Rain

Whether delicately tantalizing in the shape
of tiny droplets, or torrential in an infernal
shower from the heavens, rain comes from the
sky in a cleansing wave, sometimes refreshing,
sometimes annoying, but always wet. Post-
downfall it rejuvenates, turning up the brightness
of everything it has touched. Rain, coming from
the old English *regn*, is something we often take
for granted – even going out of our way to avoid
being caught in a spell. Yet this meteorological
phenomenon should not be underestimated.

Rain is weather's shapeshifter, taking on many
forms, from a sprinkling of barely-there
drops, to the slow and steady drizzle that
brings overcast skies. Then come the showers.
In torrents they fall, pelting the earth in a
gleaming cascade of tears, which can be joyful
and refreshing, but also all-consuming.
The earth is drenched and so are we.

Whether watching from behind the glass or
standing, face upturned to the shower, there
is something poetic about rainfall – the way it
dances off the pavement, and the cool, refreshing
feel of it against your skin; the delicate trailing
patterns it leaves behind and the way the earth
responds, quenching its thirst.

A sudden downpour exhilarates; it takes the breath away and offers the promise of new adventures, new growth to come.

Water is the elixir of life, but it also has the power to claim things: homes, objects and even lives. Our ancestors drew moisture from the earth and the sky with rites and incantations, for without it they were lost. They implored the rain gods with petitions and dances, and when at last it fell they gave thanks and revelled in the lightness of its touch. But there are always extremes, when the spirits are angered and they let their venom flow. Rain – changeable, enigmatic, destructive and beautiful. Long may it wash over us.

"*Let the rain kiss you. Let the rain beat upon your head with silver liquid drops. Let the rain sing you a lullaby.*"

Langston Hughes

The rain explained

Why does rain smell?

Rain is nature's champagne. When it falls on dusty or clay surfaces air bubbles shoot to the surface, like a bottle of fizz. These release aerosols, which are carried by the wind to our nostrils! The earthy scent, known as petrichor, lingers in the atmosphere when it rains after a dry spell.

Why are raindrops shaped like tears?

Raindrops are more like jellybeans than teardrops. As they fall the molecules that bind them together change shape – the bottom flattens and the droplet takes the outline of a minuscule bean.

What is 'phantom rain'?

The phenomenon known as 'phantom rain' happens when raindrops fail to reach the ground; instead they evaporate in mid-air, leaving a trail or wisp of cloud behind them. These sylph-like tails, which point downwards, are known as virga clouds.

What is 'blood rain'?

Since Homer's *Iliad* there have been reports of blood rain falling from the skies. While the Ancients believed that red rain meant the sky was bleeding and a sign that the gods were enraged, scientists agree that this is the work of aerial spores of green microalgae called *Trentepohlia annulata*.

Why does everything look brighter after a downpour?

Raindrops are not solely made from water. Each droplet contains dissolved nitrogen from the air, which is a natural fertilizer: this explains why grass always looks much greener after a downpour. Other kinds of rain also exist, including those of sulphuric acid or methane, which are commonly found on other planets in the solar system. Scientists have also discovered raindrops made of iron, on a planet 5,000 light years away from earth.

Why do we need rain?

Rain is responsible for depositing most of the fresh water on earth, making it an essential part of the planet's water cycle. Each second approximately 16 million tonnes of water evaporates from the surface of the earth. This is equal to the amount of rain that falls, making it a continuous and balanced loop.

Can we make it rain?

It is possible to create artificial rain. The process, known as 'cloud seeding', involves drenching clouds with external agents like dry ice, silver iodide, and salt powder. These produce ice crystals, which are too heavy to remain in the air so they fall to earth and melt along the way, producing raindrops.

How rain is made

The sun is the alchemist afoot here. Seeking out moisture from the earth, it steals from plants, leaves, oceans, lakes and rivers, transforming it into vapour that swiftly rises. Once in the sky, the vapour becomes droplets that form rain clouds. Gravity steps in at this point and the water returns to earth as rain and becomes part of the hydrologic cycle, a continual and life-giving process.

When water falls from the sky to the ground it is known as precipitation, but while you might think that rain is simply rain, there are three different types. Relief rainfall comes from the sea – as the air rises over high ground, it cools and condenses to create rain. Frontal rainfall occurs when warm air rises above cold – as the warmer air cools, it too condenses to form clouds. Convectional rainfall, which usually occurs in the tropics, is all about the heat – hot air rises swiftly, sometimes so fast that as it cools and condenses it causes thunderstorms.

Monsoons explained

A monsoon is a seasonal wind shift, which happens when mountains and highlands exist near water. As land heats up more than the water during the summer, this creates an area of hovering low pressure. At the same time there is an area of high pressure over the water. The combination causes tropical winds, which hold plenty of moisture, to form. As the winds travel high over the mountains and highlands the moist air is forced upwards, which creates thunderstorms and heavy rainfall. While this lasts through the summer months, it is often much needed – monsoons provide around 80% of a country's annual rainfall and help to maintain lush vegetation.

According to the *Guinness World Records* the worst monsoons to sweep the earth occurred in Thailand during September 1983. They rampaged through the country, lasting into the winter months, and 10,000 lives were claimed. Up to 100,000 contracted waterborne diseases and 15,000 were evacuated as a result of the devastation. More than £323 million ($400 million) worth of damage was caused.

Myths and magic

Revitalizing and restorative, rainwater is the essence of life. It gives back to the earth, feeding freshwater streams and rivers and nurturing plant life. As humans 90% of our cells are made up of water. We need it to stay alive and while most of the planet is covered by salty sea water, we cannot survive on this. The rain that falls is crucial to our existence. Like all types of weather, it is essential to the cycle of life.

In ancient times, rain was a sign from the gods. Coming down from the heavens in sheets, often with little warning, our ancestors around the world welcomed these showers. Watering and sustaining the earth and the crops, rain held mystical promise. Each drop was precious – although should it be accompanied by a thunderstorm, then it was deemed that the gods were angry, stamping their feet in a powerful rage by way of demonstration.

In medieval times the first April shower packed a magical punch. Young single maidens would collect this rainfall and splash it liberally on their face to enhance natural allure and secure a sweetheart. Farmers, too, welcomed rain, believing it would fill the cellar and fatten the cow.

Deities

Rain was the elixir of life for the Ancients. A downpour was a gift from the heavens; each sweet drop could make the difference between life and death, new growth and cracked wizened earth. Drinking water was harvested in many ways, from huge containers left to collect it as it fell, to streams, lakes and underground springs. Those early tribes dug deep into the earth to quench their thirst, often gathering ground water as it was less likely to be contaminated.

As life evolved, civilizations found new ways of collecting drinking water. The Romans built aqueducts, which transported it fresh from mountain streams into their cities, and they learnt how to filter out bacteria, boiling and letting the water rest so that particles would rise to the surface. Sand filtration columns would then allow the water to trickle through, emerging clean and ready to drink. But always, it started with those first drops of rain, which is why it was considered a precious gift from some otherworldly power. Without it, life would cease to exist.

Gentle, like the first pattering of raindrops, or assertive – the full force of a sudden downpour – deities of the rain shift and fluctuate with the seasons. For the most part they are kind of heart and giving, dowsing the earth with their life-giving essence, but what they nurture and sustain they can also spirit away.

Azer Ava

This generous Russian goddess, known as the Forest Mother, is also called 'the friendly tree goddess'. She is associated with fruitfulness and fertility and controls the rain, letting her showers fall to nourish the land. A true forest spirit, she makes her home in the trees and welcomes weary travellers and those who would come to her woods to pick berries and mushrooms.

Freyr

Norse god Freyr is associated with rain, peace and fertility. Son of the sea god Njord, and often referred to the as 'the foremost of gods', he was widely revered. He blesses the land with rain, which in turn produces a bountiful harvest, making him one of the most liked gods of old. He carries his ship with him by folding it up until it is small enough to fit in a bag, and his main companion is the boar Gullinbursti.

Mbaba Mwana Waresa

The South African goddess Mbaba Mwana Waresa lives in a rainbow-coloured house in the sky. A bountiful deity, she brings much needed rain – and when she bangs her bongos, the sky is full of thunder. A favourite of the Zulus, it is thought that Mbaba Mwana Waresa is responsible for the invention of beer. Falling for a human suitor was not popular with her fellow deities, so to bridge the gap between mortals and gods, she created beer and taught the humans how to brew it themselves. Being the provider of both water and beer makes her super popular, and even today traditional ale is made by the women of the tribe as a nod to the first female brewer in the sky.

Ua

The Maori god of rain has many titles, including Ua-Roa, which means 'long rain', and Ua-Nganga, which means 'rainstorm'. In general, rain is seen as a positive omen. A short burst of rain that quickly subsides is known as 'sacred footsteps' and is thought to be a sign that the ancestors are drawing near. It is a message from the gods, to listen intuitively and tap into ancient wisdom. In mythology the frog was thought to be a representation of the water and rain god; it was bad luck to kill such a creature, as doing so conjured devastating storms and floods.

Spirits

A violent downpouring of rain can take the breath away, obscuring your vision, making you see things that aren't really there. Your eyes try to make sense, as the water hits and splits, splashes and colours the surroundings. It becomes harder to breathe, harder to move, as each drop cuts against skin. And then you see it – a silvery sliver splicing through the darkness and you wonder, is it real or just a figment of your imagination? Such is the power of the rain monsters of old.

Slinking, sliding, cascading to earth like the heaviest rainfall, these spectral creatures come in search of life. Born of water, they move with grace amongst the land-dwellers. The Ancients welcomed the blessings of such spirits. Whether human or beast they had the power to sustain but, like the rain that switches from gentle to savage, they were far from tame. Life could be washed away in a heartbeat, should they feel the urge.

Ame-onna

Lurking in the shadows on a rainy night you will find the Ame-onna. A demon-like female spirit, she takes on the form of a wizened hag. She carries with her a bag that she uses to steal away crying infants. Her name means 'rain woman', and although she is considered evil it wasn't always this way. In ancient China, she was a highly respected rain goddess. Her transition to Japanese mythology cast her in a sinister light – although there are variations in the tale, with some suggesting she is a helpful spirit.

Mbon

These Burmese rain spirits are beings of air and are associated with nature. Traditionally they are worshipped at harvest time. It is thought that they are responsible for the fertilizing rain that waters the crops.

Nagas

The enigmatic and alluring Nagas are a race of semi-divine creatures in Hindu and Buddhist mythology. Part human part serpent, they can shift between forms and are known for their grace and good looks. They are servants to the god Indra, and as such control rain flow – they can withhold it until the eagle god Garuda forces them to unleash a sudden downpour. Thought to live in ornate jewel-bedecked palaces beneath the sea, the Nagas are believed to be the offspring of Kadru, the granddaughter of the great god Brahma. Some have a deep concern and love for humankind, while others are malevolent. Female Nagas are known as 'Nagis', and are thought to marry mortal men, forming magical dynasties on earth.

Did you know?

Rainfall record breakers

The small village of Mawsynram, in the northeastern region of India, receives the highest average annual rainfall in the world. Known as the wettest place on earth, it receives approximately 1187.2 centimetres (467.4 inches) of rain on average every year. The subtropical highland climate is responsible, with many months of rainfall and only a brief dry season.

Foc-Foc, on La Réunion island, claims the title of the highest amount of rainfall in the world during a 12- and 24-hour period. According to the *Guinness World Records*, 182.4 centimetres (71.8 inches) of rain fell during the 24 hours between January 7 and January 8, 1966. On the same days Foc-Foc received 114.3 centimetres (45 inches) of rainfall in just 12 hours – another world record, and a very wet day for those who lived there!

The small town of Unionville, situated in the US state of Maryland, holds the world record for the highest amount of rainfall received over one minute. This took place on July 4, 1956, during a powerful storm. One onlooker reported that the town received 3.12 centimetres (1.23 inches) in a minute and this was confirmed by the US Weather Bureau.

RE-WILD:
Cloud-spotting guide

Look up and gaze into the clouds. What do
you see? A fluctuating landscape that shifts
and changes with each second? A mottled vista
painted by the heavens? The Ancients viewed
the same skies with reverence; they looked to
the clouds for answers. Aeromancy, a type of
divination which looks at the shape of the clouds
along with changes in the atmosphere, was a
popular way to predict not only the weather but
also the twists and turns of fate. With ten types
of clouds to choose from, each with their own
distinctive shape and position, there is much to
see and learn from this natural phenomenon.

Clouds are grouped into altitudes, and within
each level there are different types.

High-level clouds

At the highest altitude, these clouds are thin, wispy and sometimes puffy.

Cirrus

Slender and wispy, Cirrus clouds are made up of ice crystals, which gives them a fibrous appearance. Like a spider's web, they're almost skeletal, streaking across the sky in thin tendrils.

Colour	White to pale grey
Frequency	Very common
Sky Cover	Sunny

Cirrocumulus

Small flaky clusters of white cloud, Cirrocumulus occur high in the sky, often appearing like a trail of fish scales.

Colour	White to pale grey
Frequency	Rare
Sky Cover	Mostly sunny

Cirrostratus

A thin blanket of dull clouds, appearing as a layer high up in the sky, Cirrostratus often look hazy and wavelike.

Colour	White to pale grey
Frequency	Common
Sky Cover	Partly sunny

Cumulonimbus

Cirrostratus

Cumulus

Nimbostratus

Middle-level clouds

At the middle level, these clouds tend to form in groups, rolls or layers.

Altocumulus

Mid-level cloud heaps, that clump together in rolls, they can be confusing to identify as they take on a number of forms. From tube-like twirls, to tumbling knots of wool, Altocumulus can be wavy, rippling and chaotic.

Colour	White to grey
Frequency	Very common
Sky Cover	Partly cloudy to partly sunny

Altostratus

A sheet of grey cloud that streaks across the sky, Altostratus may be bland, but has the power to block out the sun's rays.

Colour	Various shades of grey
Frequency	Common
Sky Cover	Cloudy to partly cloudy

Nimbostratus

This dark shadowy cloud brings wet weather.
While the base looks close to earth, the upper
layers stretch upwards. Thick and oppressive,
the Nimbostratus makes its presence felt.

Colour	Pale to dark grey
Frequency	Common
Sky Cover	Cloudy to mostly cloudy

Low-level clouds

At the lowest altitude, these clouds often appear thicker and darker, like storm clouds.

Cumulonimbus

With an impressive stature, and sometimes fibrous appearance, the Cumulonimbus is a powerful storm cloud, responsible for rain, hail, thunder and lightning. An anvil cloud often forms above the main cloud.

Colour   Pale to dark grey
Frequency   Uncommon
Sky Cover   Cloudy to partly sunny

Cumulus

Littering the sky in cotton wool balls of fluffy delight, the Cumulus is a gentle fair-weather cloud that comes in all shapes and sizes.

Colour   White to grey
Frequency   Common
Sky Cover   Sunny

Stratus

The bleak grey Stratus is a blanket cloud, otherwise known as fog. Dull and wavelike in appearance, it sheaths buildings and steals the light.

Colour	Grey to dark grey
Frequency	Common
Sky Cover	Cloudy

Stratocumulus

A mix of both Stratus and Cumulus clouds, this dynamic formation is the shapeshifter of the sky, and can be woolly, towering, and also layered. Thicker, and low to the ground, it's a diverse cloud and hard to pin down.

Colour	Pale to dark grey
Frequency	Very common
Sky Cover	Mostly cloudy to sunny

RE-WILD:

Harvest rainwater

Recycle and give your plants and flowers a helping hand, like those who tended the land before you.

You'll need some fine wire mesh or gauze and a container of some description like an old beer barrel, tin can or dustbin.

1. Find a spot in your garden that is exposed to the elements. If you have guttering that you can direct from your shed towards your container, then put this into position.

2. Secure the wire mesh over the open end of your container, this will keep the water clean and cool.

3. Once you have a substantial store of water, decant this into a watering can or spray bottle and use in your garden, and on house plants.

RE-WILD:
Cloud divination

It's easy to predict a gloomy rain-filled day by looking to the sky for inspiration, something the tribes of old learned quickly. A thick blanket of grey clouds is the harbinger of wet weather, and a sign to take cover swiftly, but looking to the sky to predict the future was also a popular pastime. Just as clouds are individual in their structure, so too is your interpretation of what they mean, but there are some basic rules.

Choose a clear day

Cloud spotting on a clear day is a joy and easy to do. Find somewhere you won't be disturbed, relax and, if possible, lie on the ground.

Form your question

Have a question in mind, and as you breathe deeply, close your eyes and focus on what you'd like to know.

Engage the imagination

Take yourself back to childhood, and as you look up let your mind wander, then simply wait and let the pictures form.

Take notice

Be aware not only of the shapes and pictures, but also how high the cloud is in the sky, how fast it is travelling and what colour it is.

High clouds indicate a positive outcome, low clouds mean the outcome may not go in your favour. Fast clouds suggest movement and action, whereas slow clouds suggest a longer time frame. Dark clouds tend to be negative, while bright white clouds are a positive sign.

RE-WILD:

Connect with the rain and cleanse mind and spirit

From gentle, tentative drops that trickle down your neck and windowpane, to giant, pounding showers that spray in every direction, the rain chops and changes, wets and brightens. It rehydrates, not only the earth, but you too – the way you look, the way you feel. A sudden downpour can take the breath away and reignite the spark within. Through glistening eyes, moistened from the drizzle, the world looks a different place. Reinvented, reinvigorated, a sparkling canvas, damp and ready to be painted. Embrace the power of this element and let it wash away the things you no longer need, the beliefs that hold you back and the habits that no longer serve you.

1. Put on your waterproofs and take a walk in the rain. Be bold, and brave a heavy downfall, or start small on a drizzly day.

2. Take your time and try not to rush the experience. Instead, engage all of your senses.

3. Think about what you can see, the sheen of concrete beneath your feet, or the blades of grass shining like emerald slithers.

4. What do you hear? How does the rain sound as it taps you on the shoulder? How does it feel?

5. Stick out your tongue and let the drops fall. How do they taste? Refreshing? Sweet?

6. Finally think about what you can smell and how the rain affects your surroundings.

7. When you get home, consider the experience as a whole, and how connecting with all of your senses has helped to clear your mind of negative thoughts.

THUNDER AND LIGHTNING

Thunder and lightning

If the sky were a stage, then thunder and lightning would be the headline act that steals the show. Offering heavenly drama and a plethora of eye-opening treats, this cosmic light show splits the air in two. The first billowing rumbles of thunder signal its arrival: it is the tiger about to pounce, issuing a final warning in the form of a low powerful growl. Then comes the attack, the unholy roar as it leaps upon its prey. Thunder clapping through the sky, snarling at the heels of lightning's tail.

A true spectacle for those who bear witness. To the Ancients such events would have been heart-stopping, cataclysmic and hugely symbolic – a divine message that could not to be ignored. The gods had spoken, setting their omen against a steely grey backdrop: bolts of lightning, like a mighty sword reaching down from the sky in search of a target.

Today we know the truth, and can appreciate the beauty of such a phenomenon, and yet there's still danger there. Should those spectral fingers seek us out, the touch will be deadly, so we proceed with caution, watching the performance from a distance, while some small part of us wishes we were imbued with the same power.

"Thunder is good, thunder is impressive; but it is lightning that does the work."

Mark Twain

Thunder and lightning explained

How thunder and lightning are formed

Thunder and lightning are in a constant dance together in the sky. As partners they are inexorably linked, for one cannot exist without the other. A single stroke of lightning has the capacity to heat the air to around 30,000°C (54,000°F), which causes the air to swiftly expand and this creates the booming shock wave known as thunder. Lightning bolts brighten the sky before the thunder crash because light travels faster than sound. In reality the two occur at roughly the same time, even though the dance appears off kilter.

Lightning is a discharge of electricity. This giant spark forms between the clouds, the air and the ground. A thundercloud is not unlike a battery: it has a positive charge at the top and a negative charge at the bottom. Initially the air acts as an insulator between the two charges, and the ground, but as the charges build up, the air can no longer insulate and at this point electricity is unleashed in the form of a lightning bolt. When the lightning occurs between the positive and negative charges of the cloud, this is known as 'intra-cloud lightning', and when it occurs between the ground and the cloud it's called 'cloud to ground lightning'.

Mountains and trees are prime targets for lightning's savage touch, their tips being easily within reach of the base of the thundercloud. Nevertheless, a strike can happen anywhere, depending on the random accumulation of charges.

The typical length of a vertical lightning flash is around 3.75–6.25 miles (6–10 kilometres), while the tallest strikes can reach around 12.5 miles (20 kilometres).

Myths and magic

One of nature's most amazing spectacles, thunder and lightning is a sight to behold, and to the humble human a supernatural event. Depending on your cultural background, that first clap of thunder could signify success or impending doom. Who wouldn't be mesmerized by this cosmic light show? It reminds us of the astounding power of nature, and how life can surprise and delight us with the unexpected. Those who walked the earth before us were most likely flabbergasted by what they saw, and yet they were intrigued too.

In the 1800s in Russia, a strange custom was practised to conjure the rain. Three men would climb the highest tree: one would strike two firebrands together to represent lightning; one would pour water over the branches to symbolize the rain; the third would bang upon a kettle to attract thunder!

In early Europe, church bell ringers made as much noise as possible to scare away the lightning. Church towers were common targets during a lightning storm, and even though they were holy buildings this provided no protection from the elements.

Some European superstitions claim that lightning strikes can be prevented by covering household mirrors, placing an acorn upon a window ledge during a storm, or keeping a sprig of holly or mistletoe in the house, as a charm to ward off lightning bolts.

Deities

Close your eyes during a storm and listen. Hear the first reverberations of thunder, the low shuddering echoes that fill the air, a sound so deep and filled with power that it can only come direct from the gods. Lightning rips the sky in two, another clear sign of heavenly discord. The Ancients looked to their deities in all things and believed this proof enough that the gods were making their presence felt.

While it was a common belief that thunder and lightning were divine messages, and a way of attracting attention, the true meaning was harder to decipher. Being the most boisterous of heavenly activity, it was either a form of pleasure or pain. Members of the college of Augurs, of Ancient Rome, studied the skies and used what they saw to influence political events. They believed that a lightning bolt passing from East to West was a positive omen, but one that passed from West to East was quite the opposite and a sign that the Gods were annoyed. On seeing such a phenomenon, they immediately advised that all decisions and laws should be withheld.

Baal

The Egyptian thunder god Baal was worshipped in the New Kingdom from the 18th dynasty. His name means 'lord' or 'owner', but he is also called Re'ammin, meaning 'thunderer'. To most he was lord of heaven and earth and associated with fertility, a supreme deity and master of all things. Usually pictured wearing a horned helmet, this bearded god carries either a sword, a cedar club or a thunderbolt in his raised hand. When the storms come, Baal rides the thunderclouds, but despite his might he could not defeat the god of death, Mot. Luckily he was resurrected by his sister and lover, the powerful war goddess, Anat.

Taranis

Taranis, whose name means 'thunder', is a Celtic sky god associated with thunderstorms. He carries at his side a spear-shaped lightning bolt, which is primed and ready to attack at any moment. He is also known as 'god of the wheel' – although this symbol is usually associated with solar deities, it also represents swift movement and is thought to be a reference to the unpredictable and quick nature of the storm. While his character might not appear bloodthirsty, according to the Romans he was one of three gods who demanded human sacrifice as a form of worship.

Thor

Mighty Thor is the Norse god of thunder and lightning. Wielding his enormous and magical hammer, a gift from the dwarves, he has the power to crush mountains. Just as well, as his main foes are the giant serpent Jormungand and the giants from Jotunheim. Each day he rides out on his chariot, pulled by two massive goats. These magical beasts have the power to regenerate, should they be killed in battle or eaten by a peckish Thor on his travels! Red-haired, bearded and super strong, he is one of the most popular deities, even toppling Odin off the top spot for favourite god. Thursday gets its name from Thor, being 'Thor's Day'.

Shango

The Yoruban god of thunder, Shango is a force of nature and an impressive sight. When he speaks his voice is like rumbling thunder and from his mouth pour rivers of fire. Statues of Shango often have a double-edged axe emerging from the centre of his head, a nod to his war deity status. He was the fourth king of the town of Oya and often challenged by other chieftains. After his final defeat by one such ruler, many of his followers abandoned him. In despair he took his own life, although some believe that he rose to the heavens where he was transformed into a powerful spirit known as an orisha.

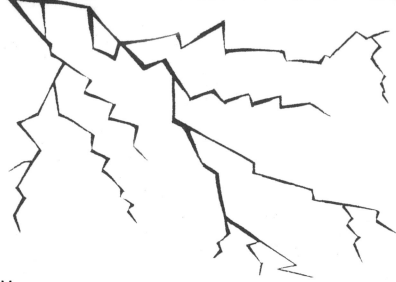

Mamaragan

Master of storms and god of thunder, Mamaragan is an aboriginal deity. When the weather is fine and sunny he lives in a puddle, but should the storm clouds gather you will find him seated upon the darkest cloud, lightning bolts in hand. When he rubs two stones together, the rain pours down. These much needed showers nurture the earth and encourage new growth.

Zeus

Taking his lofty seat on Mount Olympus, Zeus is the Greek god of thunder, lightning and the sky. King of the deities and supreme ruler, he stole the throne from his father, the Titan god Cronus. Quick to anger, Zeus dispenses judgement in the form of lightning bolts and terrible raging storms. Those who dare to incur his wrath are struck by lightning, and any place on earth that was hit by a bolt was considered sacred. Married to the beautiful goddess Hera, Zeus had many other dalliances with deities and mortals.

Monsters

With a little imagination and a magical way with words, storytellers around the world conjured tales of great thunder monsters. It was their way of making sense of this phenomenon and giving reason to rhyme. Just like the cosmic light show accompanied by thunderous drum rolls, these spirits and mythical creatures took centre stage, and still captivate us today.

Druk

Bhutan is known as the 'land of the Druk', a vast and majestic thunder dragon. Highly revered, this being soars through the air, swirling its mists around the mountain tips. When it speaks, thunder roars from the heart of its belly, and when it rains the thunder dragon honours Bhutan by calling its name. The dragon's fire appears in the form of lightning bolts, which illuminate the sky. The national emblem of the country, the Druk appears upon the Bhutan flag holding jewels to represent wealth and abundance.

Lightning Monsters

In the cultural tales of Zambia, you will find lightning monsters. These terrifying creatures descend from the heavens during a storm, upon threads of lightning. Once the thread becomes taut it will snap backwards, and the creature will hurtle up into the skies in a dart of lightning. Should the delicate thread snap the thrashing monster would fall to earth, and hunters must be sent to kill it before it can wreak havoc on the land.

Lightning Serpent or Snake

This enormous slithering beast slides a path from the heavens during a lightning storm, and when it hits the earth it produces rainfall. A key part of Native American mythology, according to Algonquin myth it was vomited forth by the creator god Manito. The Pawnee tribe believe the first rumbles of thunder are the snake hissing as it journeys to earth.

Raiju

In Japan when thunder and lightning strikes it is the work of the Raiju; these monstrous thunder beasts are entities that ride upon flashes of lightning. With multiple tails and wings they are likened to wolves, cats, weasels and monkeys, but are most likely an amalgamation of all. According to legend they are docile spirits, but the sound of thunder awakens their anger, causing them to lash out at anything in their path. Leaping from tree to tree, they thrash at the bark, leaving deep rivets where their razor-sharp claws have slashed into the trunk. Humans suffer too, and it's thought that the Raiju are particularly drawn to the navel – which explains why many Ancients wore armour to protect the stomach region. They are known to inhabit forests and woodland, so during a storm it is wise to avoid such areas. Despite their immense strength and supernatural powers, Raiju are unable to pass through mosquito nets.

Thunderbird

Making its home in the heavens, above the tallest mountains, the thunderbird is a creature of Native American legend. These giant colourful birds helped to create the universe and exist to protect and nurture the people, bringing much needed rain and storms to water the crops. When a thunderbird flaps its powerful wings, thunderclaps fill the sky and lightning bolts shoot from its eyes. Fearsome in appearance, these mighty creatures have the strength to carry a whale in their talons. Guardians of the upper world, in some legends the thunderbird would fight the Great Horned Serpent of the underworld to protect the earth from demonic invasion. Most tribes revere these sacred creatures, believing them to be a force of nature. According to the Winnebago, thunderbirds are able to bless humans with gifts and abilities. Tales from the Shawnee say they have the power to shapeshift into the form of a young boy; in this guise, the thunderbird can advise and communicate messages from the spirits, and has the ability to talk backwards. Despite being a positive symbol, thunderbirds can also punish wrongdoers – and in one legend an entire village was turned to stone because of the misdemeanours of those who lived there.

Did you know?

Record-breaking bolts
In June 2007, Oklahoma witnessed the world's longest lightning strike; it covered a horizontal distance of 200 miles (321 kilometres) and broke all former records.

The longest-lasting reported lightning strike was in Provence-Alpes-Côte d'Azur in southern France in 2012, when a single strike lasted for 7.74 seconds during a powerful storm.

RE-WILD:

Connect with thunder and lightning and step into your power

At the heart of darkness, when the earth is in the grip of a storm, there is only one solution, one saviour, that can cut through the gloom and take your breath away. Thunder and lightning ride to the rescue, super-charged and ready to explode. The fuse has been lit, and you know you are in the grip of something spectacular. You cannot deny the power of nature when you see this spectacle first-hand. It's a reminder of the spark within, the steely core of spirit that infuses you with passion and energy. The thunder is your voice, and the lightning bolt, your creative spirit. You have the power to make your mark. Be true to yourself. Say 'yes!' and tap into the energy of this phenomenon.

You don't have to wait for thunder and lightning to try this exercise, although it will certainly enhance the experience – just use your imagination.

1. Turn out the lights and plunge the room into darkness.

2. Imagine you are at the centre of a furious storm. The sky is a blanket of darkness and you can see nothing.

3. Above your head there is a clap of thunder, so loud it splits the sky in two.

4. As you breathe in, a shard of lightning flashes, sending a bolt of electricity towards you. It hits the top of your head, and travels through your body, infusing you with power.

5. As you breathe out, the lightning surges through the soles of your feet and deep into the ground, connecting you with the earth.

6. Say, 'I am strong, centred and powerful.'

RE-WILD:

Be an elemental artist

The Ancients drew inspiration from the
landscape and the changing elements, and
you can do the same.

You'll need a pen, pencils and some paper, and
a clear view of the night sky on a stormy night.

1. Get comfortable and let your gaze fall on the sky. Imagine you're watching a performance.

2. You can see the jagged bolts of lightning accompanied by the distant crackle of thunder. How does it make you feel? What does it remind you of?

3. Let any thoughts spill onto the paper in the form of doodles or words.

4. Unleash your creative side and take this a step further by turning what you have created into a picture or a poem.

SNOW AND ICE

Snow and ice

What could be more beautiful or ethereal than a landscape cloaked in snow? The glistening vista conjures an air of mystery and tricks the eye into seeing a myriad of shapes and patterns. As the temperature drops, so too does the veil between this world and the next, and there is a feeling that anything could happen. No wonder, then, that the Ancients around the world believed in the supernatural power of snow. The transient nature of this gift from the heavens left them in awe, and – while they came up with stories to explain its existence and why it fell – there was still a sense of the unknown to this phenomenon.

As alluring as the winter wonderland can be, it is also brutal and unforgiving. A place where shadows and footprints are swallowed forever, in a timeless and chilling dance. There is danger in those hidden depths, for who knows what lies beneath or how the original landscape has been transformed. From deathly snowstorms to lashing blizzards that claw at the skin like rabid dogs, winter weather comes with many challenges. What started as a captivating snow spectacle changes in a heartbeat. The twinkling showstopper becomes the spectral playground and a space where spirits, demons and deities run free, as folklore will attest.

"*Out of the bosom of the Air,*
Out of the cloud-folds of
her garments shaken,
Over the woodlands brown
and bare,
Over the harvest-fields forsaken,
Silent, and soft, and slow
Descends the snow."

Henry Wadsworth Longfellow
'Snow-Flakes'

Snow explained

Snowstorms and blizzards

Snow forms when the atmospheric temperature is at or below freezing, and there's also a little moisture in the air. If the ground temperature is also at or below freezing, then the ground will soon become covered with snow. However, if the ground temperature is above freezing, the snow falls, but melts on impact.

Snow can occur at extremely low temperatures as long as there is some moisture and a way to lift the cold air. It is a complex balancing act and a dance between warm and cold air, which can turn a gentle falling into a full-on snowstorm. When there is moist air within a low-pressure area, known as an extratropical cyclone, the warm air is forced up and over the cold air mass – but if the air near the surface isn't cold enough, then the snow will fall as rain instead. As the cyclone has strong winds circulating around it, it is common for the storm to increase in power and strength and eventually turn into a blizzard.

Lake-effect snowstorms form when cold wintry air masses flow over the warmer waters of a lake: the surface evaporates, causing convective clouds that struggle to hold all the water, which then falls back to the ground as snow. Orographic snowstorms occur in mountainous regions: the uplift of wind around the mountain combines with the cyclone to produce the heaviest, and sometimes deadliest, fallings.

Snowfall varies depending on several factors, including the speed of the storm (slower storms tend to produce more snow in one area) and how fast the warm air rises over the cold.

Snow crystals

While snow may look like a unified mass, it has many faces and facets, depending on atmospheric conditions and what happens to the snow crystals as they fall to the ground.

» Snowflakes are single crystals or clusters of crystals, which form patterns and fall from the clouds.

» Polycrystals are snowflakes made up of many different crystals, while graupel, which is often mistaken for hail, are rounded pellets of snowflake that are soft and crumbly in texture.

» Sleet, not to be confused with snow, is rain that has frozen as it falls to the ground and forms tiny translucent balls of ice.

Hail

When drops of water freeze together in a large cloud, they create hailstones. These solid lumps of ice are formed in an updraft of air, usually during a thunderstorm.

Aurora Borealis

A chilly snowscape is the perfect setting for this fabulous phenomenon, which forms when a solar flare from the sun penetrates the earth's magnetic shield and then collides with atoms and molecules in the earth's atmosphere. The reaction from this creates a coloured light show in the sky that encircles the polar region of the earth, known as the Auroral Oval. These explosions of light – called photons – are red and green when blasted with oxygen, and pink and purple when mixed with nitrogen, and they usually occur at an altitude of about 40–400 miles (65–650 kilometres).

Myths and magic

Where snow comes from

The Ancients viewed snow as a magical phenomenon. Falling from the heavens, this icy white substance had the power to completely transform the land. To the Ancient Greeks it was a rarity, but the Vikings, Celts and Romans would have been better equipped to deal with the bitter chill, having layer upon layer of tunic and fur.

In Germanic folklore, Old Mother Frost made her home in the stars. When she shakes the feathers from the downy blankets on her bed they fall to earth as snowflakes.

The Inuits and snow

To the Inuit people, the snow is what bonds their community together. It provides a sense of place and belonging, a connection to home. It is not just a way of life; it is a way of being, and they find strength in this environment. Over hundreds of years they've adapted, so that they thrive alongside the freezing conditions. Ice fishing is one of the skills that they have always put to good use. The winter upstream provides a glut of fish, which gather beneath thick sheets of ice, in preparation for their spring migration. This ancient tradition, which was once carried out with long chisels and a spoon-like tool to chip away at the ice, is an important skill, and a way of working with the elements. When the ice was eventually broken, the fish would be caught using a spear. Today nets are strung between holes, and lures with barbed hooks are used to ensnare the fish, although some still use the traditional spear, known as a kokiwog.

Snow royalty

In Finnish folklore, Snow is an ancient king who has three daughters: Thin Snow, Thick Snow, and Snow Storm. Each princess represents a type of snowflake and how it falls upon the earth.

Spirits

There is both rhyme and reason to the snow, for when it falls it provides welcome relief to the planet. The cool blanket it casts helps the earth to breathe by reflecting sunlight back into space. This regulates the temperature of the surface layer, and once the snow has melted, helps to fill rivers and reservoirs around the world. The snow, like all of nature's gifts, has purpose, and it also has poise. There's a grace in the way it drifts and gathers, brightens and thickens, that continues to fascinate with every year.

Watch the snow fall, and after a while patterns will dance before your eyes. Shapes made out of snowflakes drift and swirl, like frosted girls spinning in the distance. As the snow thickens, the shapes take on more substance, and with a little imagination, what might be a swirling spiral becomes an icy maiden sent from the otherworld to steal your soul.

Slithering between the snowflakes, her fluid form is almost translucent. She comes at the coldest point when breath is just a whisper, for she is a spirit, a snow maiden, just a slip of a girl with a frozen heart. Forlorn and abandoned, in folklore she is a tragic figure, as sweet as icing sugar, as hard and unforgiving as the frost. Her story will stay with you forever.

And so it begins, the web of tales that make up folklore around the world, inspired by nature and the changing seasons, reinforced by global events, terrible, cataclysmic life-changing acts with repercussions that last for centuries.

Yuki-onna

The Yuki-onna is a mystical entity from Japanese folklore. With long dark hair, pale, almost translucent skin and blue lips, she glides above the snow in search of her next victim. Once she was human, but the bitter chill of winter claimed her life. Now she transforms into a creature of death, a vampiric demon who steals the souls of the living. Those who see her see a maiden struggling in the snow – but it is a timeless trick, for when they try to help her they freeze to death. Those brave souls who invite her into their homes will die in their sleep. A skilled shapeshifter, the Yuki-onna can transform into fog and snow in order to catch her prey.

Snegurochka

Stepping from the heart of a Russian folk tale, the Snegurochka is a sweet young snow maiden – *sneg* being the word for snow in Russian. With porcelain white skin and sparkling blue eyes, she is the daughter of Father Winter and Mother Spring – although this varies depending on which version of the tale you read. Placed into the care of an elderly couple who cannot have children, she falls for a young boy but cannot truly love him, for her heart is made of ice. Mother Spring takes pity on her, giving her the ability to love deeply, but as her heart warms, her physical body melts. The story, although sad, is a nod to the elemental power of the snow – while delivering a salient message that it is better to live and love fully, even for a short length of time.

Mahaha

An Inuit creation, the Mahaha is a ghostly figure – thin and ravished by the cold, it looks almost human, but its blue skin is icy to the touch. With long strands of frozen hair and fingernails like splinters of ice, this being is thought to tickle its victims to death. Despite its gruesome appearance the Mahaha is not noted for its intelligence and, in most tales, those who encounter this spirit find it easy to escape from its clutches.

Monsters

Of snowy fur and icy claw, winter's beasts approach. They are resilient, able to endure the fiercest blizzards and to survive freezing conditions. The snow makes them strong and, like the flakes that mingle into one, these creatures are elusive. To some they're a frightening sight, while others might be thankful for their presence. But the real question is, did we create them, or have they always been here, hidden deep beneath the snow?

The Abominable Snowman

The Abominable Snowman, also known as the Yeti, draws upon the snow for its power. Making its home in the Himalayas, this savage man-shaped creature is clothed from head to toe in thick fur. According to the Tibetan Lepcha people the idea originated from a hunting deity, which appeared as a strange human-hybrid mix living amongst the snow. Those in the area who practised the Bon religion laid claim to a ferocious humanoid, whose blood was used in magical rituals. Whatever the roots of this tale the core truth is a lesson in safety, for the Yeti is used as an example of the potential danger that lurks in the snowy mountains of the region.

Dance of the spirits

A light show sent from the gods, the Aurora Borealis manifests in the Arctic and Antarctic areas, with the whirling lights providing a stunning backdrop to the ice and snow. Breathtaking to behold, it was named after the Roman goddess of the dawn, Aurora, and the Greek word for the north wind, *boreas*. The Native Americans call it the 'dance of the spirits', while the Vikings believed the phenomenon was a message from the gods, and a way of highlighting the path to Valhalla, where Odin was waiting to feast with the chosen ones.

Barbegazi

In the French Alps, on the border of Switzerland, lives the endearing Barbegazi, a tiny fey being, similar in appearance to a dwarf. Its long white beard is strewn with icicles, which is where the name, meaning 'frozen beards', comes from. Covered in a thin layer of white fur, the Barbegazi has enormous flat feet, which it uses like skis to navigate the slopes. A friendly creature, in tales it helps those lost in the snow and gives avalanche warnings – although it has a liking for the latter, and enjoys surfing the falling snow. Thought to live in a network of caves beneath the mountains, you will only catch sight of the Barbegazi during the colder months of the year.

Frost Giants of Jotunheim

Jotunheim is one of the nine worlds of Norse mythology, which are connected by the branches of Yggdrasil, the World Tree. A world of eternal ice, cold and snow, it is inhabited by the Frost Giants – huge fearful characters that plague the realm of the gods and humans. Being born from the cold, a deluge of snowfall and extreme weather follow in their wake – which could explain the heavy snowstorms and blizzards of the time!

Deities

When snow falls, the vista changes in a matter of minutes. Dark and rugged becomes a sliver of brightness, a gleaming blanket to blot out what went before, and because of this many ancient tribes believed that snow had the ability to cleanse and replenish. The dramatic dip in temperature coupled with the terrible weather conditions meant that snow was also seen as a harbinger of doom and gloom and a symbol of death to some. Storytellers of old would have looked to the land for their cues, and created epic tales of the gods' wrath to explain this dark magic, hence why so many legends and monsters were born.

And so, like magic, they arrive out of nowhere. Blanketing the world in brilliance, they lay their snowy cloak on the ground. The light they cast is sometimes fleeting, and sometimes so bright it takes the breath away. Snow deities have a power that walks the delicate balance between good and evil. They bring beauty, devastation and change.

Aisoyimstan

This Native American god, whose name means 'cold maker', is found in tales from the Black Feet people of Montana. Appearing on an ivory steed, and dressed head to toe in white, he blankets the earth in frost and snow wherever he goes.

Cailleach Bheur

Associated with the coming of winter and the snow, and the cycles of life, Cailleach Bheur is a deity of Scottish tradition. Battered by the elements, she appears as a blue-faced crone – but don't be fooled, this goddess oozes power and was often petitioned for strength over adversity.

Chione

Sprinkling flakes of snow from the heavens, Chione is the beautiful Greek goddess of the snow. Daughter of Boreas, the north wind, she was a favourite of the god of the sea, Poseidon, with whom she bore a child.

Morana

This Slavic goddess of death and the winter is much feared. Her appearance is never a good sign, for with it she brings harsh weather conditions, including snow, ice and snowstorms. She usually appears as a wizened old woman, but for those who show no fear she takes the guise of a beautiful young maiden – although this is no consolation, as it's usually the last thing they see before death!

Skadi

A giantess and Norse goddess of winter and the snow, Skadi is most famous for avenging her father's death at the hands of the god Odin. Storming the fortress in Asgard, she demanded justice, but instead was offered the hand in marriage of one of the gods. The catch was that she had to choose her suitor by only looking at his feet. Having a crush on the handsome Baldur, she plumped for the prettiest looking toes, only to discover they belonged to the god of the sea and wind, Njord. As expected, the marriage did not last long!

Around the world

There are many different words to describe snow, from terms and phrases, to more descriptive names. Every language has a word to capture the spirit of this weather phenomenon, but these cultures have several. Here are some of the main ones.

ICELANDIC

Hjarn – icy snow

Kafsnjór/kafaldi/kafald – deep snowdrifts

Krap/slabb – slushy snow

Mjöll – fresh snow

Snjór/snær – snow

INUIT

Aputi – snow on the ground

Aniu – snow used to make water

Kannevvluk – fine snow

Maujaq – snow which you sink in

Muruaneq – soft deep snow

Pirta – snow blizzard

Qanik – snow falling

Qengaruk – snow bank

SWEDISH

Aprilsnö – snow in April

Åsksnö – snow during a thunderstorm

Kramsnö – snow that can be shaped into snowballs

Lappvante – thick falling snow

Modd – snow that is slushy

SCOTTISH GAELIC

Blin-drift – drifting snow

Feefle – snow swirling around a corner

Flindrikin – a light snow shower

Glush – melting snow

Skelf – a large snowflake

Snaw-broo – melted snow

Did you know?

Snowiest place on earth
Aomori city in Japan is the snowiest place on the earth. Situated at the highest peak of the Hakkoda Mountains, it receives 8 metres (26 feet) of snow a year. The thick fog that surrounds the city is known by locals as the 'snow monster'.

RE-WILD:

Create a snow sculpture

Express how you feel with a snow sculpture.

You'll need a pile of snow that's not too dry and powdery. A slightly wet substance is easier to mould and shape.

You'll also need tools to carve, such as a wooden spoon, a chisel, and an ice-cream scoop.

1. Start with a compact pile of snow and work from the top down.

2. If you have a specific concept in mind it's a good idea to have a sketch to work from. If not, simply enjoy the process and let your imagination take over. This doesn't have to be perfect – it's a bit of creative fun.

3. Add a fine spray of water as you work – this will help the sculpture stay firm.

4. Decorate your sculpture with some colour or glitter, or simply leave it white, bright and fabulous!

RE-WILD:

Connect with the snow
and find inner peace

There's a stillness to the landscape when the air
is thick with snow. As those flakes start to settle,
the earth becomes muffled, as if wrapped in a
tight white duffle coat. It is softly smothered,
and although icy to touch, there's a warmth here,
a purity and timelessness. Snow makes you want
to snuggle up close, to pile on the layers and get
cosy, but it also offers you the chance to have fun
and experience the thrill of the icy chill. Wrap up
warm and venture out. Watch others having fun
and share in the beauty of a wintry vista.

Every living thing leaves a pattern in the snow,
from the tiniest of mice and birds, to the
bounding pawprints of a dog running riot.
It's time to make your mark and connect with
the natural world.

1. Put on your woollies and your wellies
   and take a walk outside. Find a patch of
   untouched snow and launch yourself into it.

2. Sink your feet deep into the mound then get
   creative and use them to make a pattern,
   or draw a face, or a smile. Do what comes
   naturally and give your imagination free rein.
   Take deep lungfuls of cold air as you work.

3. Hop, skip, roll and dance, use your hands,
   your arms, any part of your body that feels
   right, then take a step back and admire the
   masterpiece you've created. Feel a sense of
   peace roll over you, like a fluffy blanket
   of snow.

Final word

Wild, wonderful, and sometimes weird, the weather has it all. It's an integral part of our experience upon the earth, and it's forever changing, moving with the challenges of the times. It cannot be tamed or controlled as our ancestors discovered, and while we might attempt to understand it, we can never really know what comes next. The weather is unpredictable, as history illustrates, but while some events seem out of our hands, there is much we can do to channel the positive effects of the climate, from harnessing different types of energy, to working with the gifts of each season. Yes, it demands our attention and respect but it also delights, lifting the thoughts of the day, and making each moment memorable.

When we think back to a cherished memory, we recall the season, the nip in the air, the sweet scent upon a spring breeze, or the dishevelled snowman that we made from the first falling of snow that winter. The weather sets the scene and helps to transport us back through time. It brings colour and meaning to life, and while we might bemoan it on occasion, we would be lost without it.

Over the years, elemental events have reshaped the structure of the earth, but always there's a sense of renewal, as we adapt with the landscape. The weather, like a gifted sculptor, carves the world we live in. Today, as our climate shifts and changes, we wonder what is in store for future generations. We plan and strive to change global warming, to consider the rising seas, and the energy we use that affects the earth. We do our bit, but sometimes all we really need to do is be aware of the natural world and the transitions of each season. To take inspiration from those who lived hundreds of years before us, who worked the land and had a deep relationship with the environment. Taking each day as it comes, and living in the moment, we can return to what is truly important.

We can learn to connect to the elements and tune into their life-enhancing power. It matters not if the sun is blazing brightly, or the sky is set for a storm, there is beauty and grace in both events, for each is a meteorological miracle.

The weather is our companion as we journey upon this earth. Always a revelation, often unexpected and unannounced, think of it like an old friend – a guide to help you understand your connection with the natural world, and where you might fit within it.

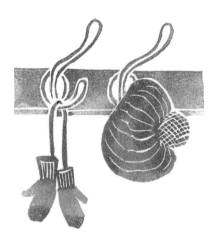

"Sunshine is delicious, rain is refreshing, wind braces us up, snow is exhilarating; there is really no such thing as bad weather, only different kinds of good weather."

John Ruskin

Index

About the author

A professional storyteller, with a keen interest in the natural environment and folklore, **Alison Davies** enjoys delving deep into the myths and legends that have shaped the world today.

Alison is the author of over thirty books; she also runs writing workshops at universities across the United Kingdom.

Acknowledgements

I would like to thank the two wonderful editors who helped to shape this book and bring out the best in my writing – Stacey and Harriet – the A-team!

I would also like to give a big thank you to Clare, for her fabulous illustrations, and Gemma, who designed the book – their combined artistry has worked its magic with my words.

Publishing Director
Sarah Lavelle

Senior Commissioning Editor
Harriet Butt

Editor
Stacey Cleworth

Senior Designer
Gemma Hayden

Illustrator
Clare Melinksy

Head of Production
Stephen Lang

Production Controller
Sabeena Atchia

Published in 2021 by Quadrille,
an imprint of Hardie Grant Publishing

Quadrille
52–54 Southwark Street
London SE1 1UN
quadrille.com

Text © Alison Davies 2021
Illustrations © Clare Melinksy 2021
Compilation, design and layout © Quadrille 2021

Cataloguing in Publication Data: a catalogue record for this book
is available from the British Library.

ISBN 978 1 78713 625 0
Printed in China